This
BE(E) EMPATHETIC
book belongs to:

_____

GRATEFUL

Be(e)-ing **GRATEFUL** means recognizing someone has done something nice for you.

All you need to do is....

BE(E) HELPFUL.

BE(E) THANKFUL

Showing that you are GRATEFUL
is easy to do.
It makes people happy which will
make you happy too.

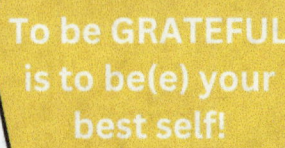

To be GRATEFUL is to be(e) your best self!

Being **GRATEFUL** is easy to do. Can you give an example of how you showed gratitude today?

What did you do recently that made you **HAPPY**?

Flip this book over to read **Story 4.**

Read **Volume 1** to get two more stories about what it means to **BE(E) KIND & BRAVE.**

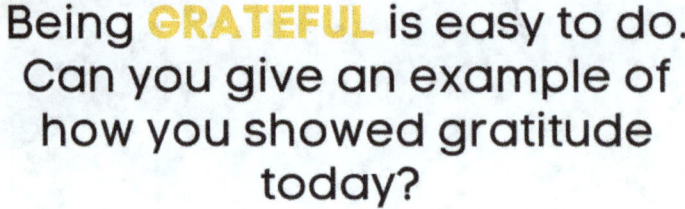

www.wrdplay.co

Check
out more
books at
wrdplay.co

EMPATHETIC

ISBN 978-1-998025-49-7

W_RDPLAY

Flip the
book over
to read
Story 3

By feeling good and having fun you
will spread **HAPPINESS.**
So, be the best YOU can BE(E).

BE(E) PLAYFUL.

BE(E) POSITIVE.

BE(E) EXPRESSIVE.

HAPPINESS

Be(e)-ing **HAPPY** is about feeling good and enjoying yourself with great friends...and of course family.

All you need to do is....

This
BE(E) EMPATHETIC
book belongs to:

_____

www.ingramcontent.com/pod-product-compliance
Lightning Source LLC
Chambersburg PA
CBHW081016120626
46546CB00010B/3173